FROM DEATH TO LIFE

DEVOTIONAL

Shareé Jackson

The information in this book is true and complete to the best of our knowledge. The author and the publisher disclaim any liability regarding the use of this information. Books and media by Sharee Jackson are available for special premium and promotional uses and for customized editions. Imprint Productions, Inc. can bring Author Sharee Jackson and other speakers to your live event. For further information, please email info@imprintproductionsinc.com.
Cover and Interior Design by RED Media Group,
a division of RED Worldwide, Inc.

ISBN:978-1-7358124-0-3

Manufactured in the United States of America
10 9 8 7 6 5 4 3 2 1
Library of Congress Cataloging-in-Publication Data is available
Copyright © 2020 Imprint Productions, Inc.
Jackson, Sharee.
From Death to Life
ISBN: 978-1-7358124-0-3

DEDICATION

I would like to dedicate this first devotional to all my girls: Kalyssa, Bae'lee, and Najerriona; Son-in-law Curtavious Gainey Sr.; grandsons: GJ, Adonnis, Seven; and granddaughter Selena; step-son Bode; and last, but not least, my wonderful husband, Saliu, whose name means "man of great wealth."

Thank you all for your encouragement and motivation as we prepare to launch this amazing devotional.

Shareé (Beautiful Flower)

TABLE OF CONTENTS

From Death — To — Life

The Son Has Risen

Death And Life Are In The Power Of The
Tongue...
Life Or Death.

I Am The Vine!
You Are The Branches.

FROM DEATH — TO — LIFE

But the fruit of the spirit is love, joy, peace, forbearance, kindness, goodness, faithfulness, gentleness and self-control. Against such things there is no law. (Galatians 5:22-23)

"Of all of these listed above, the most important one," answered Jesus, "is this: hear, o Israel: the Lord our God, the lord is one. Love the Lord God with all your heart and with all your soul, and with all your mind and all your strength."(Mark 12:29)

The second is this: love your neighbor as yourself there is no commandment greater than these. (Mark 12:31)

See the law is summed up into two simple commandments. Love the Lord your God with your whole heart, soul and mind-- and if you do he will give you strength. (Galatians 5:14)

And he also requires that we love our neighbor as we love ourselves and we have taken the first step in the right direction.

Without love we have not God and if we think we do we are deceiving ourselves.

"Choose to take a change in direction on today. Love the Lord thy God with your whole heart, mind, body, and soul. And love your neighbor as you yourself

"LOVING GOD AND LOVI NG YOURSELF"

Love can change the whole course of a person's life. God says" by my loving kindness have I drawn thee. So we are to exhibit the same love to others as the father showed us. If we put love into practice we can make the world a better place, one smile at a time.

Take this challenge from today going forward. Vow to smile, hug, or give a high five to at least one person a day and see what this little act of kindness does for the one you exhibit it to as well as how it makes you feel...... that is the love of God. Make one person smile and it will intern cause you to smile.

Choose today to walk in love. As we come outside of ourselves, and how we perceive things and let God show us the need of others. And as we become willing and obedient and let the "homeless Jesus," come in and use us as His mouth, hands and feet--He will become to us all we need.

Be about the father's business and he will be about ours. Let go of self today. Pick up your cross, and let the love of God lead, guide and direct you.

The steps of a righteous man are ordered by the Lord.(Psalms 37:23)

"LOVING GOD AND LOVING YOURSELF"

Ways in which I demonstrate my love for God / Ways in which I demonstrate love for myself:

_____

_____

_____

_____

_____

_____

_____

_____

_____

_____

_____

"HATE KILLS"

Hate is one of the world's silent killers. Once the seed is planted, it sets in and takes root. once planted, it grows like wildfire. It kills dreams, destroys families, and it separates you from the love of God. His word says, how can you hate your brother whom you see every day, but say that you love me, whom you have never seen.

There's no way you can love God if you don't love your brother or sister, for God is love and if you have not love, you have not the Father.

Love is patient, love is kind, love holds no accounts of wrong. (1 Cor. 13:4-8) so my brothers and sisters, repent. Ask God for forgiveness and allow Him to show you His true love. Be not deceived. The devil comes to kill, steal and destroy. Take your life back by placing it in the hand of the Lord. Surrender and tell the devil who and whose you are. If you are a child of the true and living God, you will seek and pursue love. You will no longer be led by hate, instead you will be led by the Spirit of God.

MY STORY:

2 Words that describe who I am or who I am becoming:

_____

_____

4

SALVATION

Salvation is achieved by simply believing. The word says, they replied, believe in the Lord Jesus, and you will be saved-you and your household. (acts 16:31)

So by you believing confessing salvation does not just help you. It saves you and your family. See there are people that are connected to you. Once you get in position, those connected to you are positioned with you. We are called to be trend setters.

See we are to be examples. And once we walk into our true calling, God opens up doors for us and others as well. The word says, as for me and my house, we shall serve the Lord.(Josh. 24:15)

The only way that can happen is to let God come into our lives, and

Transform us, and let Him live through us.

They will wonder how we went from the way we were to the way God will change us to be. That will cause them to want to change also. Be that bible, let people read the love of Christ in you.

MY STORY

Name 1 way you see your salvation impacting others?

_____

_____

_____

_____

_____

RENEWED

Transformation comes by the renewing of your mind. That is another step to true salvation. We can't come into the presence of the Lord full of filth and dirt. We have to lay it all down and be transformed as well as renewed.

The word says, you can't put new wine in old wine skin, because the rips and tears will allow the new wine to escape.

But when you become transformed and renewed, and your wine skin becomes new, you then are able to receive and hold all the newness of God.

He saved us, not because of righteous things we have done, but because of His mercy. He saved us through the washing of rebirth and renewal by the holy spirit, whom he poured out on us generously through Jesus Christ our savior. So that having been justified by His grace, the hope of eternal life. (Titus 3:5-7)

MY STORY

Which areas of your life do you desire renewal?

_____

_____

_____

_____

_____

FAITH

Faith comes by hearing and hearing the Word of God. See it is by faith that we believe. Because we have never seen Christ, so we go off of what we feel is right. But you have to be careful. There is a way that seems right. But in the end leads to death.

So in all the things, pray, pray and pray. Seek God with fervor. That we seek things that means us no good.

The Word says, walk by faith and not by sight. So what we see is subject to change but what we can't see is what is set in stone.

In all that you do, put your trust in the Lord. Have faith that He will do all that His wonderful Word proclaims that He can do. Without faith, it is impossible to please God. (Hebrews 11:6)

MY FAITH LIST

List 7 things you are believing God for?

_____

_____

_____

_____

_____

BE COVERED BY THE BLOOD

Jesus was the sacrificial lamb that he sent into the world to live among us, and perform many wonderful miracles. Whom God sent to die for us to save us from our sins.

I thank God that He loved us that much to sacrifice His Son for me and you. God demonstrates His love for us, while we were still sinners,

Why I am most thankful His blood has covered me:

Christ died for us. (Romans 5:8)

He did that to be a blood covering to cover us from our filth. To forgive us of our sins.

So, therefore brothers and sisters, since we have confidence to enter the most holy place by the blood of Jesus, by a new and living way opened for us through the curtain, that is His body. (Hebrew 10:19-20)

Lord thank you that by your blood, we are covered!

MY STORY

Why I am most thankful His blood has covered me:

_____

_____

_____

_____

_____

DELIVERANCE

My chains are gone, I've been set free, my God, my Savior has rescued me. Like a flood, His mercy came. With endless love, amazing grace……

When deliverance comes, with it comes change. When you are truly delivered, you are free.

For His word says, whom the Son sets free, is free indeed. (John 8:36)

MY STORY

What I am being set free from:

_____

_____

_____

_____

_____

PEACE

My peace I leave with you; my peace I give you, I do not give to you as the world gives you. Do not let your hearts be troubled and do not be afraid. (John 14:27)

See, the peace of God surpasses all understanding, but the ways of the world brings troubles and heartache. (Philippians 4:7)

Where does your peace come from? Does it come from the Lord, or from the world?

Choose today whom you will serve. When you make the right choice, you will have a joy from deep down inside. If you choose the world, you will continue to be in a constant battle. You will find no rest.

True peace only comes through Jesus Christ.

Come to me all who are weary and burdened, and I will give you rest. Take my yoke upon you and learn from me. For I am gentle and humble in heart, and you will find rest for your souls. For my yoke is easy and my burden is light. (Matthew 11:28-30)

If we choose to pick up the burdens of the Lord because they are light and the yoke of the Lord for it is easy, things will become so much easier.

Nothing in the world can give us peace or rest, lest it is given to us by the Father. Let's get our focus right!

This is how I will use peace in my surroundings:

_____

_____

_____

_____

_____

_____

_____

_____

_____

_____

_____

_____

_____

_____

Come Follow Me

Your Faith Has Made You

Whole

A True Relationship

Die To Self... Live In

Christ Restoration &

Reconciliation

COME FOLLOW ME!

Then He said to them all, "whoever to be my disciple must deny themselves and take up their cross daily and follow me. For whoever wants to save their life will lose it, but whoever loses their life for me will save it. (Luke 9:24-25)

God requires something from us. He requires that if we are gonna live for Him, we have to die to self. that means all the things that we want, how we want to live and even the way we think, we have to lay it all down.

God is waiting for you! Will you lay down your evil ways, and die to self? Will you pick up your cross and follow Jesus?

If you choose to follow Christ, you cannot begin to imagine the things that will begin to change in your life, and the joy you will discover or the hope he will fill you with.

If you continue to choose to walk with Satan our adversary, you will continue to have heartaches, failures, disappointments, as well as failed dreams, and failed relationships. We will not enter into the rest and peace that our souls, hearts, spirits, and minds so desire.

MY STORY

A few areas where I need God's help:

_____

_____

_____

_____

_____

_____

_____

_____

_____

_____

_____

_____

_____

_____

CHOOSE YE TODAY LIFE OR DEATH

PRAYER

But when you pray, go into your room, close the door and pray to your Father, who is unseen. Then your Father, who sees what is done in secret, will reward you openly. (Matthew 6:6-8)

Prayer is the most essential key to unlocking doors. Once we come to realize that our Father is just a cry away, we will come to have a true relationship with Him.

He desires to hear from us, to commune with us. He wants us to spend time with Him.

The time we spend talking to friends, watching, playing games, and etc. He wants us to be as eager to spend time with Him as we are to do earthly things.

Come to Christ. I pray that you begin to have a new hunger, thirst, and zeal after His righteousness.

His word says, seek first the Kingdom of God and all His righteousness and all these things will be added unto you. (Matthew 6:33)

Today is the day to get a new fire. One that will purify the soul, cleanse the mind and place a renewed spirit within you.

Learn to take everything to God in prayer. When you get the urge to call someone about a problem, give our Heavenly Father a chance first. Take all things to Him first in prayer. You will be amazed at the outcome as well as how fast God responds.

Some things will take longer than others. But remember good things are worth the wait.

MY PRAYER

_____

_____

_____

_____

_____

_____

_____

_____

_____

_____

_____

_____

_____

_____

Remember, do not be anxious about anything but in every situation, by prayer and petition with thanksgiving. Present your request to God. And the peace of God, which transcends all understanding will guard your heart and your mind in Christ Jesus. (Philippians 4:6-7)

HE IS RISEN

Whoever believes in the Son of God accepts this testimony. Whoever does not believe in the God has made Him out to be a liar because, they have not believed the testimony God has given about His Son. And this is the testimony. God has given us eternal life, and this life is in His Son. Whoever does not have the Son of God does not have life. (1 John 5:10-2)

This is a promise that we can hold on to. Whoever has the Son, has life.

But if you have not the Son, you have not life. The best gift that was given to us was the blood of Jesus. God sacrificed His Son that we may live and have life abundantly. God says: you are my Son, whom I love, with you I am well pleased.(Mark 1:11)

Live a life that is pleasing to the Lord so that when you come face to face with our Father, those words, He will speak to you.

The Lord looked down from His sanctuary on high. From heaven He viewed the earth to hear the groans of the prisoners and releases those condemned to death. (Psalm 102:19-20)

This is a promise that we can hold on to. Whoever has the Son, has life.

But if you have not the Son, you have not life. The best gift that was given to us was the blood of Jesus.

God sacrificed His Son that we may live and have life abundantly. God says: you are my Son, whom I love: with you I am well pleased. (Mark 1:11)

Live a life that is pleasing to the Lord so that when you come face to face with our Father, those words, He will speak to you. The Lord looked down from His sanctuary on high. From heaven He viewed the earth to hear the groans of the prisoners and releases those condemned to death. (Psalm 102:19-20)

Release any and everything that is holding you captive and allow Him to renew you and set you free!

FREEDOM

We are free to do anything, but not everything is profitable for us. What are you doing with the freedom given you by our Lord and savior?

Are you using your freedom to profit the kingdom of heaven? Or are you using your freedom for selfish gain?

There is a way that seems right to man, but in the end leads to death (destruction). (Proverbs 16:25)

But the ways of the Lord are good and there is no wrong that can be found in the ways of God. He is the author and the finisher of our faith. (Hebrew 12: 2)

His word is true. If we just take some of the freedom we used to put up with, do and try all types and manners of evil, towards reading and spending time in His word, we will come to know true freedom.

We will then begin to lay down, let go of, and grab hold of the true principles of freedom.

God's ways are not our ways, nor are His thoughts our thoughts. Neither has it entered into the heart of man, the things that God has in store for us.

Come to know Christ and find the keys to true freedom!

And watch what God unleashes in your life.

Freedom the right way is amazing. There is no feeling that I can humanly explain to you.

But I encourage you to try Him for yourself, and let the freedom of the Lord do a great work in you.

Study the word, then you will know the truth and the truth will set you free! (John 8:32)

And if the son sets you free, you will be free indeed! (John 8:36)

Because, through Christ Jesus the laws of the Spirit who gives life has set you free from the law of sin and death. (Romans 8:2)

Name 1 way you see your salvation impacting others?

_____

_____

_____

_____

_____

_____

_____

_____

ROCK OR SAND

So when the storms of life arise, how will you respond? Will you be like the house built on sand or like the house built on a rock?

The house built on sand will sink when the storm comes. But the house built on a rock will endure the storm.

Trials come to do two things. To shake us or to make us stronger. You know that when things get the hardest and we become weak, that's when the Lord stands up in us and shows us His strength. Without the Word of God hidden in our hearts, we are sure to fall. But if we draw from our source, we will be able to endure.

Satan comes to steal, kill and destroy. But the Lord comes that we may have life and that more abundantly.
The word says that the one who hears my word and puts it into practice is like that of a wise man who has built His house on a rock. (Matthew 7:24)

But it also says that, one who hears my word and does not put it into practice is like a foolish man who built His house on sand. (Matthew 7:26) Will you be the wise man, or the foolish man? God is waiting to do so many great things in and through you.

Apply the word of God to your life. Don't be just a hearer of the word but a doer as well.

So when the storms of life arise stand firm and rely on the Lord and he will help you withstand all the trials of life.

Do not be afraid, little flock, for your father has been pleased to give you the kingdom. (Luke 12:32)

When circumstances arise, I will:

_____

_____

_____

_____

_____

_____

_____

_____

_____

_____

_____

_____

_____

_____

UNDERSTANDING

Trust in the Lord with all your heart and lean not on your own understanding; in all your ways submit to Him, and He will make your paths straight. (Proverbs 3:5-6)

So many times we fail because we rely on the understanding of ourselves and others. Most of the time we don't seek God first.

But seek first the Kingdom and His righteousness, and all these things will be given or added to you. (Matthew 7:33)

See, God knows our needs, our wants and our desires and he is ready and willing to give them to us.

He's just waiting on us to bring everything to Him first in prayer.

Blessed are those who find wisdom, and those who gain understanding. (Proverbs 3:13)

And when we begin to seek Him first, He says "before they call, I will answer; while they are still speaking I will hear . (Isaiah 65:24)

So when we get an understanding and put first things first, we activate the hand of God and He begins to move on our behalf.

He loves to bless His people.

MY STORY

Help me to understand:

_____

_____

_____

_____

_____

_____

_____

_____

_____

_____

_____

_____

_____

OPEN DOORS

See, once we line up and get in the will of God, He will begin to open doors that no man can shut, and He will also close doors that no man can open.

God has many doors that He is urging you to walk in. Blessings upon blessings.

God knows just the right time to close and open doors on our behalf.

He is never early or never late. He's always on time. What doors need to be shut in your life? And what doors need to be opened?

MY STORY

Praise you, Father, for opening doors for me:

_____

_____

_____

_____

_____

_____

_____

FORGIVENESS

So, watch yourselves. If your brother or sister sins against you (Proverbs 27:5-6) rebuke them; and if they repent, forgive them. Even if they sin against you seven times and come back to you saying I repent, you must forgive them. (Luke 17: 3-4)

Unforgiveness is one of the biggest things that holds us back. Unforgiveness causes sickness, headaches, pain, seizures, etc. It is a vital key to our deliverance. We must forgive in order to receive forgiveness.

We must repent and ask God to reveal any hidden unforgiveness in our hearts that would cause us to not be able to come before His throne of grace with our requests.

Because His word says, therefore; if you are offering your gift at the altar and while there, you remember that your brother or sister has something against you, leave your gift at the altar. First, go and be reconciled to them, then come and offer your gift.(Matthew 5:23)

See, in order to even approach our Heavenly Father there are things required of us so that what we present to our Lord will be heard. When we forgive, our God has something he wants us to know.

MY STORY

Oh, Father, help me to forgive:

_____

_____

_____

_____

_____

_____

_____

_____

_____

_____

_____

_____

_____

THAT WE OURSELVES ARE FORGIVEN

Blessed is the one whose sins are forgiven, whose sins are covered. Blessed is the one whose sin the Lord does not count against them and in whose Spirit is no deceit. (Psalm 32:1&2)

Now faith is confidence in what we hope for and assurance about what we do not see. (Hebrew 11:1)

MY STORY

Father, forgive me for:

_____

_____

_____

_____

_____

_____

_____

_____

_____

_____

RIGHTEOUSNESS THROUGH FAITH

But now apart from the law, the righteousness of God has been known. To which the law and the prophets testify. This righteousness is given through faith in Jesus Christ to all who believe in Jesus Christ. To all who believe there is no difference between Jew and Gentile. For all have sinned and fall short of the glory of God. And all are justified freely by His grace through the redemption that came by Christ Jesus. God presented Christ as a sacrifice of atonement, through the shedding of this blood-to be received by faith. He did this to demonstrate His righteousness, because in His forbearance He had left the sin committed beforehand unpunished. He did it to demonstrate His Righteousness at the present time so as to be just. And the one who justifies those who have faith in Jesus. (Romans 3:21-26)

MY LIST

Father, here are those with whom I want to share my faith:

_____

_____

_____

_____

_____

_____

_____

ABOUT THE AUTHOR

Shareé is the first sibling of three children; her late brother-Vincent and her sister Kaprisha. She was born to Marcus Crawford and Lisa Moffett in Wichita, Kansas on June 15, 1981.

Shareé is passionate about winning souls for the Lord. She desires to share inspiration on how to pray, how to read the Bible, and how to surrender your life to Christ. Sharee has inspired so many people during her journey. She loves encountering new people and never sees anyone as a stranger.

Shareé was inspired to produce this devotion as an easy read and illustrations of how we can simply enter into a relationship with God.

Shareé wants everyone to enjoy the freedom and the simplicity of the relationship with the God.

Shareé currently engages in projects that will supply various needs for people that are challenged in different situations. She is a public speaker and a licensed cosmetologist. She is involved with advocacy work and mentoring.

www.ingramcontent.com/pod-product-compliance
Lightning Source LLC
Chambersburg PA
CBHW041624110426
42740CB00042BA/44